CRAIG STERRY POEMS

CRAIG STERRY POEMS

1965 - 1974

Charleston, SC
www.PalmettoPublishing.com

Craig Sterry Poems 1965-1974
Copyright © 2023 by Craig Sterry

All rights reserved
No portion of this book may be reproduced, stored in a retrieval system, or transmitted in any form by any means–electronic, mechanical, photocopy, recording, or other–except for brief quotations in printed reviews, without prior permission of the author.

First Edition

Paperback ISBN: 979-8-8229-1811-5

DISTINCTONS

First Prize, All University Poetry Contest,
Michigan State University, 1967
Hart Crane 7 Alice Crane Williams Poetry award, 1970
Newburger Poetry Award, University of Oregon, 1972

PUBLICATIONS

New: American and Canadian Poetry
Caravel
Chelsea
Fiddlehead
Road Apple Review
Pebble
Southern Poetry Review
The Goodly Co.
Wormwood Review
Apple
Caravan
Tennessee Poetry Journal
Epos
Quartet
Quixote
Red Cedar Review
Hearse
Lillabulero

For Diane

That night in my dream you were crying
and someone spoke up and asked is death this close?
and i woke and found you crying
and the house locked up like a tomb
and gas hissing from the stove
and i threw the window open
and the moon slid down my arm, pale and older,
and in the street a cat was turning hot circles
and the room sighed its dark poisonous breath
and we slept again, and the small red eel
slipped out from our eyes to dream of loss,
traveling the distance between us, through mudgrass and
reeds that tangled underfoot
and we wondered how long will it take.

And i woke again, or did i wake?
to someone tooling copper or leather,
pounding out belts and bracelets below us,
or was it only the englishman's wife hammering steak?
and i sat in the chair with my hands underneath me asking
how long will it take?
but the day took up its pounding too
turning everything fiercely white
leaving whatever it passed the same
asking us please to sit and wait
for noise to dream of silence,
for darkness to ask its only question over and over,
first to the hands that hid beneath us

and then to my legs cramped in a false and bloodless sleep,
and wait i did for the smaller noise of bone against gristle
to carry me sleepward part by part, shoeless, backwards,
finally to idle in sleep's finest clothing, in the deepest
slowest, dreamless brain and back again, to sound's recovery,
leaving the silent, whispering half-dark like a woman lifting
her skirt to walk in sand, toward the knocking of the daily engine,
the sun's aluminum rattling sea and whining wind, the clattering,
imaginary chains wishing to be broken and single again,
as everything resists the law that holds it together,
longing for erosion as all things long to erode to their seperate
and final place, like a shoe
washed up on the beach, the single feather dreaming its aimless,
noiseless flight, back to the sleep that unites each part
from the other – deaf and unable to speak.

So as if the sun says sleep if you must, I sleep where it leaves me
and dream that my father plays the fiddle and sings
and i travel again, in no direction, leaving my baggage,
and the man in the next seat dies
and the driver says see how easy?

And I continue by jet, a silver needle piercing the moon,
asking myself is this possible?

And by mule, not knowing where, wondering what have I done,
finally to stand at this door with my boots in my hands,
Banging off the mud.

                                          Published in *Poetry Now* 1974

At Night Through A Pennsylvania Forest

This darkness is thick
as sleep. My wife has deserted me
for the back seat, tired of talk.
The radio mutters and whimpers like a dog
dreaming. Even the engine drowses, hums
to itself.
In this place where the only light
comes splintered through branches
from a low moon, I could be taken
by surprise, could be driven
face to face with things I tend
to disbelieve. Like flying saucers
or the cloudy faces of ghosts
or, around some curve on this easy forest road,
death, caught in the headlights
like a startled deer.

Epos   A Quarterly of Poetry 1968

Storm

The wind blew all night
And half the day
My wife and I lay in bed
Afraid to look from the windows
At the ruined crops.

At noon we sat down to eat.
Columns of steam rose from the wreckage
Of vegetables and meat.

Tonight the wind is a drunk
Asleep in the fields.
Our house is taking root.

Lillabulero 1969

Cowper's Ravine

Above me an explosion of birds—
Air hums with a misery of afternoon heat. . .
  Lying in high grass by a fern-dark marsh,
  where moose stumble to suck at their reflections,
I watch my hands, moist and speckled
In the light like trout. . .
  From Cowper's Ravine
I hear the bells of guns—the execution
Of illegal grouse. . .
  I lie in high grass
My head soft as an ant's egg. . .

Lillabulero 1969

I Am Walking In A Field

My boots fall behind each other.
they leave dark words that go back
to the road, to home, to myself leaving for a walk,
my day of work, breakfast and waking,
my wife's moist buttocks, back through
years of sleep and the shoes
of fifty people
to the first pink grubs of my feet
kissing my mother's bed.

I leave the scrawled trackings—what I
failed to be.
What I will become
lounges ahead in the air.

I walk the doubtful promise of my flesh.
The endless rumors of my feet
will talk me back to the earth.

Lillabulero   1969

In The Bearpaw

1.   He fishes Jim Creek.

A trout—

it tries to swim, even in a man's fist . . .

It would say:

I came here by accident
from a high snow lake
I fell along this boulder creek for miles
to where you are . . .

But the mouth only swallows a warning
to the gills:
air, air, air!

2.   He Calms His Pack-Horse

Those mountains to the north
we won't climb them . . .
They belong to men who cause avalances, rockslides . . .

They live inside the trunks of trees . . .

When we take the trail at night
You'll hear them whispering . . .

3. He Breaks Camp

This morning a beast leaned over a pool to drink . . .
I saw it was me . . .
I saw through the black holes of my eyes
my black brain.

Lillabulero 1969

Metamorphosis

It was then that we were babies –
Heads too heavy, hairless,
Boneless, beautifully
Ugly, touching
Life softly
In cheek and breast.

It was then that we were boys –
Eyes filled with worlds
That never went past Baker Street
Or Cameron Hill
Where we skidded down
The snow-packed troughs
In cardboard boxes,
Or played combat with broken slats
When spring came.

It was then that we were lads
Or punks
Or whipper-snappers –
Heads empty, hair too long
Driving cars that spit our anger
Through straight-piped manifolds,
Tasting cigarettes and beer and
Girls too soon women, in the darkness
On top of Cameron Hill.

It was then that mothers cried
Until they fell asleeep, dying a little.

It is now that we are men,
Or nearly so – afraid of ourselves
And of others
And of the cold,
Sleeping with heavy wives
Who often cry
After midnight.

College Poetry Anthology 1965

Looking At My Hands

Below my window
the uncertain headlights of bicycles
search the streets.

From the RR yards
engines and boxcars rumble
coupled in agreement.

On these nights
my poems turn away from me
like cold women.

The Fiddlehead 1969

Meeting Marcia

Looking at the ashtray
and tearing napkins into bits
stunned the air between us
into a wound
until

risking her embarassment
I touched the back of her neck
and by so doing
thought her into a frail glass swan
my grandmother
once showed me.

The Fiddlehead 1969

The City

I walk long tunnels
of warm air. Read the paper, think
I knew a girl who died. See the fire engines
slinking back from false alarm.
Watch the secretaries
skinny as grasshoppers.

Cities pinpoint my strangeness
my clumsiness. That feeling
of waving to someone
you don't know.

The Fiddlehead 1969

At Home

My hands are small animals,
undoers, meddlers in silence,
ruiners of food. . .
Cups cringe from my winding fingers
Like women from unwanted lovers. . .
Books holler and leer in crowds. . .
Rain chuckles on the streets. . .
The bed, old whore, contains me
apologetically. . .

The Above Ground Review   1968

Cross Country

At dawn, our plane got up
And turned its sulking wings East
Towards noon. . .
Below us in Montana a lookout tower
strained to see threads of smoke
against impossible odds. . .
Inside, a firewatcher listened without moving. . .

Later, as Chicago circled below us
(the engines and I serious
with the business of descent),
the firewatcher thought about Missoula
down Swan valley and south
over mountains
a thousand miles high. . .

The Above Ground Review 1968

One Day

Late that spring when the ice was
Breaking up along the Milk, we walked –
Old Anderson and I – to the top of Prairie Hill
Where some Indians once stopped to rest or hunt
(I preferred to think they stopped for battle),
Leaving proof of their visit in rings of stone
That once held down the tipi's edges.

He knelt, and as he smoothed the young grass,
He talked of other rings of stone on other hills
Long since picked and piled by fences
When the sod was busted.

Then he pointed to a spot
Where he once found an arrowhead
(I could hear it whistle and "thunk"
As it hit a trooper in the back),
Which he kept for a while in a
Dresser and finally lost.

These were the last hills, he said,
And these, the last rings of stone.
(It was a perfect day for baseball)
And someday, he said, (the wind would be
Blowing straight to center field)
They would be gone.

It is hard to remember
Everything he said.
He was an old man
And the sun was out.

That afternoon I flew my kite
Right smack into some power lines.
It tangled and I pulled too hard
And broke the string. It hung there
Rattling for days.

Caravel: A Magaine of Verse   1965

After Searching Until Dark
For a Wounded Deer

When I reached the door
The trees were humming like tuning forks. . .
Earthworms curled deeper down than roots. . .
All night the forests marched through my sleep
Like Russian armies searching
For lights. . .
Leaves rattle, sharp as accusations. . .

I had taken to the roads to find a city,
The knife sheathed in my hand
Blinking with
Every step. . .

Tennessee Poetry Journal 1969

Stopping Through

Maybe the flatness
of the empty road or
the empty radio
drove me among foreign streets
to find your unlit steps
suspect of stray dogs
and town cops.

I should've run:
the doorbell went berserk as
a fire alarm, startling your
house with lights;
and once begun,
our talks lurched like heavy kites
making the best of a small wind.
Your wife, surviving
the emergency, went
back to bed.

Leaving the interstate at dawn,
I locked the sun in the rear-view mirror
and melted your town into butter.

NEW: American and Canadian Poetry 1968

Leaving Dark Rooms

Through the orchard dawn pushes up.
Smudge pots cold. Crook of oak. Barns
fading red. Boy dawdles in turnips.

Road to the city. In the flats, on the wide
Parchment earth, enduring heat.
Night. Faces in wood. Enamel moon.

In the city, cinematic, the racket of labor.
In the harbor, sandstone dusk, cool wash of air.
Border of ocean. Men line the boulevards, wave
their ragged coats. Ships go by pulling
the ocean behind them.

Sun dark scroll. Workmen scrape their tools.
Midday delerium.   Walk the streets
dreading the beggar.

Sun's glint. White Algerian beach. Coast at my back.
America breathing down my neck.
Sundial moves a rusty spine, a face turning,
seizing the light.

Sun painted into a corner. Seamstress in the window sleeps.
Dog in rags. Beyond the reef white castles of yachts.
 I dream of the ship that will haul us.

Curtains flow back. Night jasmine.
Rolling in a sheet, hunkering dreams.

In my life the lady walks, scooping diamonds
From the street, flinging them down. She is no common
girl.
Roots settle, autumn ore. Bird becomes a song.
Fish in hand, rummaging the currents, reaching
Under rocks.

Down a doughy road, clay cottage, pencil smoke.
Boredom of wonderland. Standing in the open door,
wind pouring overhead. A pressing toward
some vauge urgency. Rhythm calling rhythm.

Careless June. Noiseless tossing wind.
Sky an old chart. In the bush, thin river.
In the west, unsettling hills.
Birds on imaginary winds. River with a bridge
In its lap. On the pilings
dark bags of crow.

Through the trees colorful birds. We alone unclothed.
In the animal's eyes a certain light. Our dreams
are not strong enough. We pick through stone.

River of night. I walk without a trail.
Across a pock of meadow, the half life of the moon.
I catch my feet falling into the throats of gullies.

Footbeats on the path. Voices in the forest.
The mad river's laughter.
I walk the foothills, through spindling pine,
prairie falling back on the easter curve.
I think of the city. Along the streets
the survival of youth.

This morning my dreams restored
of sea lions coming to watch me on the shore,
a blue sea house with broken stairs.
On the balcony, young girl.

Sun through fog. I remember the ocean.
Children of the family. Kodak yellow.
July in garden pants. Ophan Annie eyes.

On the farm. All day
in the field it is morning.
We lose nothing.

Sky swollen. Hills grown brown.
Feet on cool stones.
Summer emerges.

II: Forest

One day lends me to the next.
The coal bin is empty space.
In the kitchen skulls of ladles gleam,
tall black hats of pots.

Darkness leans its back against the fire.
I lie in bed unfinished, hear you
Stuffing drawers.

Outside it is October's wind and sheetrock sky.
I come to my senses. I know the nights are
growing tails. I walk along the only road.
Cedars clutch and wail. I feel the full
cold air.

The forest is without emergency,
sky stretched flat out.
Tonight on the bed, the odds
and ends of a month. I have added the days
like planks in a raft, like skins
to a heavy coat. On horizons
cities are burning.

I am standing at the edge of a forest
that I cannot see. Across the cross-patch floor
the riveting of light. At home you are
eating pistachios, taking tea from bone china,
playing your piano of ivory and oak.
On a stump I sit like a jug.

Darkness clinging, moon drilling the nights.
Then for days, abiding the rain, you stand
in the hallway, without confusion, hearing bells.
Steam rises from the cup. Cold has nailed
the windows shut. Fog has overthrown us.

The rain sweeps in 3 days
the river rolls past its banks.
Caught by the storm I walk along
the blur of path. A deer
or a dream of one. Forest path
or the dream of all paths and similar rain.

Morning gone again. Feet cold as the dead.
I wake to myself like a coat I no longer put on.
Full of forgotten addresses, a sack of old schemes,
directions all wrong.
Sun cracks up the clouds,
the insensible rain.
This where we live. So
this is where.

Under the rind of moon, November's cruel touch.
The shabby frames of mountains, of failing health.
Sound of a windowless house.
In the yard, sound of horses.

Under the tree, pits of the promised fruit.
Under the house, cats in a trance.
Above the clouds, the constellations turning
on their smooth brown heels.

Tonight the wood is wet clean through
thinking whether to burn. Tonight the moon
is passing through our lives, hiding faces

of amusement and concern. Tonight
the mother wearies of her child.

Ionosphere burns the planet blue.
A strange wind that blows in all directions,
wheezes through the house to snuff the lamps,
batters the door like an animal.
From the window I creak across the roof,
piss on the shingles.

III: The Ocean

A cold Monday, down to earth.
Up the streets of the community
shops open, slow rain quickens the feet.
The mill buries itself in sound.
Behind us all day, the vast
Immunity of ocean, flocks of birds.

Rain pivots the fence.
The dogs whine against their leashes.
Foghorn wanders in the fog.
She stares at her hands, the smoke.

Windfall across the roof.
Moonlight slices the bed. A lamp goes on,
she rolls to her feet.

On mountains illustrious with snow
birds topple off to sleep.

In the first cold blast of winter
I have fogotten
the sun will raise me from the dead
to stuff me in my socks.

Morning's kettledrum procession.
The town resumes under the eyes
Of the law.
Afternoon. I sleep in a strange room.
Outside, rain is being read aloud.

It is still night.
Shadows sink into the pavement.
Dark houses, dark houses,
live by the churchbell sea.
Something invisible falls to the floor.
Lost dogs come home.

Winter is coming on iron wheels.
It is the shape of things.
The year is wearing through.
I jig my way home.
The moon watches
in dead suspense.

IV: Leaving Dark Rooms

Your pull yourself from sleep,
A swimmer hauling out.

Day takes direction under a worsening sun.
Thunder in the regions of storm. Seed tosses
in the wind. The garden holds in rows.
Down the halls of corn, you go kneeling
in the weeds.

As the river goes
over the rubble
through the wreckage of bridges
darkness settles the animals in its lap.

You hold yourself, your feet turning
the earth underneath. You eat and the dog eats.
You walk and the sun goes down behind you.
You stand and all your days stand end to end.

On Tuesday you draw the curtains
to the grass growing through the fence,
the old woman stooping in her flowers.

Animals gather. No one speaks.
You search for the perfect apple.
You stand on your head, your pockets dribble pennies.
The dark climbs out of a hole.

Heating the soup
You twist the bottle in your shirt.
Philosophical booze talk.
Shit of the ages.

The old man sips wine, says he never
had shoes, broke padlocks for food.
You run.

Who tells you all they know?

Hours go unnoticed
leaving day-old bread.
You ask for the time
change for a dollar
the truth.
You think. Something to remember.
Anything.

Leaving dark rooms, you crack your foot
against nothing. You nudge the door.
Lights go on and on.

You leave and return again Exhausted
you say without thinking.
Yes.

You watch from the window
a city retreating in alleys and smoke.
You go walking, all the gesturing in air.
You long for the prisoner's brief escape,
that true momentary joy.

V: Sleep

Thunderous clouds.
Winds above the city.

Your father writes from home,
It was a high-sky day.

You settle down. The business
of sleep. Time used up behind you,
talk of quick solutions.

You dream each rung of a ladder
to the top of a creaking spire, the wind there.
Ocean limply around your neck, rising
To wherever you climb. The rope heaved over the wall
Just catching.

You dream. Your fear of the falling stair. The innocent
Murderous gun. The warning. Red rain from a red sky.
The lock on the door.

You dream. Cosmonaut Leonov hugs his wife goodby.
November shuffles hollow-faced.
You walk on empty fields.

You dream. Laying down the shovel and walking off the job.
Walking off the job whistling.
You dream. Watch the weeks sway past like fish.
Last of the wages.
You dance the calypso,
Goats in hell.

Whatever in sleep fetches you back
pushes your arm its certain length.
You come back complete.
A skater skaing his 8.
You take a place in line.

VI: Snow

Ghost snow crosses the road. Onto the frozen lip.
White dog crosses the field. Birds come nervously
to take the corn. The stubble waits to take up
its life again, in the burning cold, in the brittle
hickory woods.

The dog moves down the hidden fence, suddenly uplifting
        Birds---
past strongbox houses, past the town's edge, where the dead
are given their cross and stones.

Through leagues of snow
over the cold expressionless ice
you come home, take the cat's chair.

The light fails. You draw closer.
In the fire, pictures of the explosion.
Logs burning like battleships.

You move to the light.
You tend to the living, water in the flowerpots.
They return to you
their brief displays of joy.

Wind rumors. Dim bells ring.
You follow your steps not thinking.
They lead you here. You lie down
by the stone. You give your ears
to the dead. They say nothing.

You search the edges for a new start. Walk aisles
crammed with goods. You come home,
knock over the cup,
watch the candle's slow collapse.

Imagine gaining time, you smile
from room to room. Outside, that color blue,
water seizing back to ice.

Dawn. Purest sound, as light escaping,
plunges soundless. We are a crowd
roused up to cheer.

You go with your child
over frost in the courtyard
holding out your arms to the slow
return of light, the wind. Whatever is coming

Whatever is at hand.

Poetry Now 1974

To A Suicide

This was different
the way you might hear a sound
on the floor of a desert
or the heart just before sleep
  cabbage in its old sack
  holding everything. . .

In the city
doors locked themselves
and the weakest buildings tremored
and clutched their addresses . . .
From the windows the moon
Blossomed in rows on your teeth . . .

Southern Poetry Review 1972

Montana Visit

I

Bearded relatives I never knew
burrowed into the moonlike landscape,
actually made things grow,
and when it got better they
called out wives from the East
who ate potatoes and grew thick and
inarticulate each year dragging babies
from childhood as though childhood
were some kind of sickness.

The sons stayed scared by tradition
take stairs now one at a time
are stiff in the cities they visit
would rather walk than ride.
And their sons
live like businessmen from the town
cajole the same ground
their tools in bright colors
lace on their boots like
delicate instuments
kiss their thin city wives
and coax grain to grow in such
grade and quantity that it
bends the father in shame
like an old spoon.

Now I come here a visitor
foreign as the government
guilty as a sailor bring back
a new disease.
It is my going that infects
will empty out their beds and chairs
tranforming all their new machines
to old dispairs.

II

Already there are
aunts in Seattle
cousins from Oakland
who never come back
except for funerals.

And there is evidence
from talk in the bars
that even the seasons may not continue
responsibly, may shift
and be lured by strange facts
of gavity
pulling the rains to the deserts of Nevada
Or Mexico.

III

I have come back for reasons of desperation
to repay desperation.
I will be the stone, picked and flung
and followed

as others followed what was flung
to this place.

Going will be given
by those who stay
and it will be taken by those who go
cautiously as the arms of mothers
teaching sons
to dance.

Lillabulero 1970

Dream Poem #1

I was driving north
in Canada
in a bus full of different friends from my life
going north to fish
and when I stopped along a huge lake
we saw pieces of debris
hitting the water . . .
We watched. . . it was a plane, about to crash . . .
It wobbled and struck the water next to the shoreline . . .
I took off a heavy wool coat, my arms getting stuck
in the sleeves . . .
Lloyd Vilett, a school friend,
followed me . . .
We swam to where the plane should be
dove down, the water warm,
lifted the craft by the tips of the wings,
took it up to the road . . .
It was suddenly diminished . . . the size of a toy . . .
I opened it and took out three tiny figues—a man
and two little boys . . . they were pink like plastic . . .
I pushed their small stomachs, water came out their
   mouths . . .
I breathed air down their throats, they became smaller . . .
They woke, lay wriggling in my hand
like baby mice.

Wormwood Review 1969

Margaret

Upstairs in her room
   she gracefully dances
the newest dances
   with the tallest men . . .
staggers the air with perfumes . . .
chews bits of True Romance . . .
   adjusts her mirror . . .
sighs . . .

From where she lies
sandwiched in a garden
of printed sheets
   she swears once a week
she hears a man's breath
   leaking througth the window
glimpses him flashing away
   from tree to tree . . .

Pebble: Volumn I 1968

Undocumented Observations from the Letters of G

In the marrow of the living
families mourn their dead
and in their deepest part
even greater families
mourning . . .

It's discovered
This has been going on
For some time now
in the simple arteries of ants
in the unsteady skulls of tortoises
making the bones dark and heavy . . .

This is best seen
when birds
are suddenly afraid
of falling.

Quickly Aging Here
Anthology: Some poets Of The '70s

Thinking of Our Visits

Coming back and
coming back I am
watched by your children
whose eyes are green as
a Mallard's head
and you, blending smiles with your medieval wife
and those Mexican girls you keep
Dancing hysterically on your curtains.

Thinking of our visits
breaks panic from my blood at night
Like a covey of pheasant . . .
This clock I own
now grinds me through its teeth . . .

I am boney as a knuckle
and sick of my mistakes
knowing even sidewalks keep themselves alive
with names and dates.

My friend, it's this: I'm sexless now
without the names of wife or child,
awkward as the piano
that sits
in a widow's home.

Unpublished

Distances

Day gone over the hill
the crow goes taking everything
hammers of industrial neighbors
chainsaws tearing through myrtlewood
horses in the straggled fir
distances walked in bad shoes
shadows crossing the table
a spot of light the cat left
room smelling of fish.
Didn't we leave as full of plans against the dark
as the crow flew
clicking his beak like a small wooden box.

                              Unpublished

Under The Man

The night swings above him
like a bell. Metallic blue.
Stars like crushed glass.
He is on the old creek bed. The dead river.
His feet are fishes rising
and sinking.

An owl, angling its wings for food, goes down the dry white corridor
over the glad bones of fish.

Under the man the river walks backward
into its life, goes mad climbing rocks,
becomes snow. Becomes the storm.

The dying lake flies to the owl
holding itself in a dark bowl.
it is scattered with stars.
it floats the moon.

                                              Unpublished

Untitled

Daylight's grand illusion
hopless as the terms of love
and prayer thin.
Nothing fears so much
as dark laid back.

The boys come from the dead
Hollering in chorus
I listen to my voice
Seething but will not sing.

Fame would kill me sooner
than whiskey or money.
That much I'm sure.

Please desire
This goddamed need that
Pours from our hands and feet wanting
Everthing at once

                                                   Unpublished

Should We Banish the Moon

Should we banish the moon from our poems
the moon that knows the whereabouts
of all dogs.

should we finally throw the moon in the fire
where all the rest of our poems will eventually go
the color blue cooing with it like a fake gem

shall we banish the whorehouse moon to its place
among the empty bottles and tinfoil
letting it be content
to coo its name over and over to itself

should the moon be thrown like the stone
that has dulled on the mantle
should we consider only moonless nights
and give the dark no reference

even if the coin is moon-like
glowing dimly in the deep pocket
even if the fingers touch it thinking moon
Still we will write no poems that
mentions its name.

PRAISE FOR CRAIG STERRY'S POETRY

"His poems have a glittering boldness and a total authenticity."

Galway Kinnell
Pulitzer Prize 1982

"His poems have a ring of authority, a sureness and control one would hope to find in a writer of any age."

Charles Wright
National Book Award 1983
Pulitzer Prize 1988

Craig Sterry is *"... possessed of an original and profound vision of the world."*

Ralph Salisbury
Oregon Poet Laureate
Professor Emeritus University of Oregon

Craig's poetry was contained in the collection *Quickly Aging Here: Poets of the 1970's.* In the author's notes he wrote the following about himself:

I spent the first twenty years of my life living on and around my father's wheat farm in north-central Montana. Took a degree in English from a small teacher's college. Worked as a farm laborer and a RR telegrapher. Went to Michgan State Unversity for a graduate degree in American Literature and quit. Joined the Merchant Marines and quit. Tried editing a little magazine and quit.

I started writing when I was about 19. Kept at it without a real sense of commitment till I was 23 or so. Which is about the time I gave up on graduate school, threw out my old poems and started over.

www.ingramcontent.com/pod-product-compliance
Lightning Source LLC
LaVergne TN
LVHW092100060526
838201LV00047B/1484